Sketches of My Life

Tiffany Heard

Sketches of My Life
Copyright © 2021 by Tiffany Heard

Library of Congress Control Number: 2021904311
ISBN-13: Paperback: 978-1-64749-395-0
 ePub: 978-1-64749-396-7

All rights reserved. No part of this publication may be reproduced, distributed, or transmitted in any form or by any means, including photocopying, recording, or other electronic or mechanical methods, without the prior written permission of the publisher or author, except in the case of brief quotations embodied in critical reviews and certain other noncommercial uses permitted by copyright law.

Although every precaution has been taken to verify the accuracy of the information contained herein, the author and publisher assume no responsibility for any errors or omissions.No liability is assumed for damages that may result from the use of information contained within.

Printed in the United States of America

GoToPublish LLC
1-888-337-1724
www.gotopublish.com
info@gotopublish.com

CONTENTS

Introduction.. v
Chapter I 1
Chapter 2... 5
Chapter 3... 11
Chapter 4 17
Chapter 5.. 23
Chapter 6..27
Chapter 7..31
Chapter 8..37
Chapter 9.. 43
Chapter 10 49
Chapter 11.. 53

INTRODUCTION

About what god see yourself as god see your life

How do you see yourself pause for a moment?

And think about it what thought have you had about yourself today?

So many of us find ourselves basing our self-worth on how I used to give

Upon myself and I used to always get put down and

When I was in my room at Valle vista I started to think about

How God has changed me and how I will not allow the devil to come back and take over my life

I am a survivor of the bad thing that has happened to me

I will overcome my hard time

I started to think about how god has changed me

CHAPTER I

When I grew up I had a hard life being a child, I was always being mistreated by my family they never cared enough about me, but talk as though I wasn't there, but it was ok, I never knew that I will be a success in my life. When I was a child I was alone in the dark by myself because I was just a child, it was Ok, so when I was there it was okay that I always like to be by myself, my family called me slow and crazy I was beaten by my mom shoveled into the corner, but it's ok I will always be the thing in my life, I tried to deal with people because it was sad just too tired of stuff. I had to go through stuff because I want to. But not good just maid to them because I just do what they want as I grow up. I always had to do what people ask. I could do enough on my own, I was always asked or told to do something, that's why walls gets put on people, I was never shown love all my life. I had difficulty with family, men, and people because, not even once in my life I was ever loved. I had so many blows to my head and body, it was not funny, I have always lived in the dark, I didn't have any friends, but it's ok, just life always want to be like and love, when a year went by, I still did what people told me to do even when I was a child so each day I learned how to take control of my life, I always ask God, Why me? Why do people harm me? Why me Lord? Why am I alone in this life? I don't have anybody to talk to or befriend, with you it's sad, but you have to keep going, just living, finally, found a friend they are alcohol and drugs, one of them now come with personality changes because street got you, then experience all kind lifestyle situation then hear go jail mental health place because can't get together then got called slow all type name called them you got called slow all type called them you weird folk in the world just care about people just one of them.

When life passed you by, you start thinking like people in the street, act like them too because you have nobody in life to guide you to the right way that Parents should raise their children to raise them right so they don't go wrong.

Go be messed up like tiffany were being raised from street allows for experiences of all kind of thing, you must make choices in life.

Once upon a time in my life,

Just want the best for tiffany I am tired struggled one month to another. All my life never have enough people always taken from me my grandma on my dad side left the house for my sister and brother my dad's family taken the house and money from us but it was ok we still live, I and my brother got the worst end of all, but all said and done tiffany got the worst of it all, nobody cared about her at all.

How would you feel to be locked outdoor? Can't come to the house to daddy, be outside for a couple of hours, hungry and thirsty but it live thoughts all, but my mom had a problem that she would fix, Lord just tired of it because it was bad to me I'm tired of this mess, it's just too much because just not in god will lord trying so hard deal with stuff but it hard just explore world think to be good so I hoped for a better life for myself.

I struggled along time I had escape thing in my life forget better I had to fight with people just have placed too stay but it ok I had hard life not ashamed of because in the world. In a lone dark room with nobody to talk to. People always close a door in my face, but it was ok. I tried to do my best with people. Lord I'm tired of this messy world, it's just too much because people find me difficult when I am too tired to seek God for myself I hope and pray that it be all right because just not in God's will, the lord trying so hard to deal with stuff,

But it's hard, people get alcohol in them they start to yell at you because they're just drunk, it's ok because I'm just tired of the mess, how can I understand? Why do I have to deal with it? I'm not going to deal with it anymore because there is just Satan in him, it's all right just live in God's hands. So please God help me. Though when I didn't have anywhere to go, two boys in the rain saw my mom outside, told her to sleep there in the living room.

It was ok because we didn't have anybody my mom had a small apartment with one of my child and sisters children stay there too, but I tried my best to be together but it wasn't proper at all, me and my boy used to sit at the library when it gets dark we didn't have anywhere to go it was sad because when they try to deal with a family member they letting down it ok.

I hoped that one day we wouldn't be living like that anymore because it was sad in your case, you didn't have any more help because turn back to me and my boys we been in the cold trying to survive in this world, but we keep going to jail for stupid stuff when I was younger, but it was ok, We made mistakes in life in pay off it just want to continue to bless me in life lost everything in storage but it ok to people gave lot stuff we lost all be hornless but it ok we made it through the grace of god.

I'm grownup, I have children that I couldn't raise because I didn't have money and a house to put them in, I didn't know how to raise children, but all said and done I still love them. Just could do it because I didn't grow up in a perfect family home, but I made it through life, I got with the wrong crowd and started to get in trouble, do drugs but I'm not ashamed, it's just an experience in my life I had dodged people because they just leave me alone. I didn't have anybody to talk or play with when I was a young lady because so where locked in my room or lock outdoor on the porch till dad get home. I didn't have what my sister and brother. I had to take and run with it all my life. I wanted to own a house, a nice car and a swimming pool in my backyard. They all dream but hope that god will reveal all that to me because I'm tired of struggling with my life. I want everything. I want to go on a trip, to explore the world. But its ok I hope that I get my wish when I try hard in life when I can be living the good life when I was a child and since growing up I hoped that give full blessing to me. I hope with a prayer that I receive it because I did deserve better in life. I hope one day be send my book too prison for lady. In their show them long journal of process but seek god will it will be bless to you.

CHAPTER 2

I Tried So Hard

I tried so hard, I tried my best
I gave you my all and now there nothing left.
You have stolen my heart then tore it in two, now I'm falling apart and don't know what to do.
Divided by decision burned by the fire, confused by your words.
Tempted by desire, I'm living in the past not knowing what I'll lose, not Knowing what will last, blinded by fear. Drowning in doubt, I struggle to be free looking for a way out.

Hebrew 3-9

Know it in my book, I put in my book. so bear with me you should be good for yourself I should put that in no book for you read you all know it in my no book for you read own words now to live in this world honestly people always distract you what try to do god will even man or husband always got some to say about you but long no god for yourself enough seen matter too you all ask god teacher how to live in dis world not be ashamed in life that wrong with worlds now because we have wisdom and knowledge at all worries the lord tried stopped my crying because it hard for me deal with man always got game for you so I will hardly be a good woman to him. So I tried so hard to do my best and help people, but it's not me, but its ok I just ask the Lord to help guide me with this book. Because I am ashamed of my life. I hope one day I will be living a good life and be happy, and stop living in misery out because it is just a trip so just I'm sad and cry out to god not helping me. I didn't have a good childhood and most of my adulthood life because I had a man treat me so alone in the dark. I hoped for a way out. I keep seeking god's words when I was a little girl. My mom was always mean to me, always shout out a lot of things, beat me, never had mom love me like everyone else. She always shovels me to the side and I was picked on in school and high school. I never had anybody to like me. i was always alone by myself nobody to talk to but hope for a way out. To shout out a lot of things. Beating me made me learn how to take care of myself never had a mothers love like everyone else. She always shouts out a lot of things. Beat me. I'm always by myself nobody to talk to but my sister then my dad got tired.

When a year went by I still did what everything people tell me to do. I still did what people told me to do even when I was a child so each day I learned how to take control of my life.

I always asked god why me? When people do harm to me why me Lord? Why me? I have such a bad life. When I'm all grownup people do harm me why me Lord? Why do I have such a bad life? When growing up I was alone in life I didn't have anybody to talk to or be friends with. It's sad but you have to keep going just living finally, find friends they are alcohol and drugs and then one of them then now come personality change because street got you then.

Then I experienced all kinds of lifestyle situations. Then hear go jail mental health place because can't get together then got called slow all type name called them you got weird folk in world just care about people just one of them know how it feels to be locked outdoor. Can't get in the house till my dad comes home, then your mom beats you half to death, what can I say? Just as a child, my mom broken up a lot of my toys and clothes, then brought me to be mistreated by man and use me. But its ok think of god's law thing happened in my life, it's ok to think of god's law, it ok to still live, to still seek god words.

I hope and pray that god gives me a breakthrough in my life and maybe one day I will be successful in life, I am tired of junk. I had to go through with man.

Lord bless me with my own house that I can call home. That is all I ask for. I seek you, king, that I get my own home that I can call tiffany house where I can keep the people that tell me to get out away. Lord step in for me please all I ask is to help me get my own home because I am tired of being put outdoor.

Lord help me because I'm tired of this stuff because it is the devil who tries to attack me. I ask of you please help me in all my circumstances because I'm not worthy, I just want to finish my book and live my life to the fullest. Does goodwill tired of cry with the mess I'm in, shield me because I have a good heart. I need to stop letting people mistreat me calling me slow and crazy. It's ok I'm just tired of stuff because it's too late to try and find my life. My life in God's words keep me with a sound mind, the devil wants me to break, but I will not my lord I am declaring victory over my life and not let the devil step in. because it wants me to be afraid. God, I hope for the day that I will be successful in life because I want to stop worrying about what people think I just want a better life for myself because I'm going to get better with it. People want me to look stupid but I'm not all my life I want my own house, a nice car, and a swimming pool in my backyard. They are all my dream, but I hope that God will make my dreams real and talk to myself about the thing I tired of the struggle with my life, I want everything, I want to go on a trip, to explore the world. I wished to try hard to get my book published so I can be living a good life when I was a child and since been grownup I hope that give full blessing to me I hoped that God has received my prayers because I do deserve a better life. I hope one day sends my book to prison for a lady in there, to show them a long journal of the process but seek Gods will it will be blessed to you by God.

It sad when you been used by people, when you think your friends is for you are not just tired of try be people please I just want be alone living my life just tired of people tell what to do I try to make mend with my children that didn't happened so mad with me about this man I am with, but I'm a little sad about it now. Time for me to live for me and not nobody else. I might have had to leave that man be with my children and grandchildren.

I am tired of being a slave for people doing what they say because they're old. I'll go on with my life stop holding me back. It's got to do with my life so help me please because I need a change in my life Lord from the people not being better with it I want to do my dream and finish writing my book, Lord I'm tired of this mess it just too much because once people get alcohol in them they start to yell at you. I'm just tired of this mess how do I get myself in it. I want to explore the world. I just pray that I get peace in my life and my family turn back to, but its ok ill just deal with it soon, God give me a breakthrough because it's terrible to ask god why me? I don't understand why I got to deal with it not going deal with anymore because it's just Satan in him it all right just live in god hand so please god help me through this difficult storm.

Sometime you tired stuff people do to you hope one day I will be success in life I just want to live normal life be happy I stay out of damn and stress so just tired I hope that people seek good in me not bad my children don't have enough with me because I put man for them my mom said I am real not in her marriage she beat me so bad it just anybody mess it ok just world I am still seek god will do it will to death put want on career when I say did something in my life I keep pressing through it because it get hard when everybody turn back on you. I hoped and prayed that I get a breakthrough with my book. I'm confused in this world, its ok to still hold on to my world and Gods words but when it gets hard I just get tired sometimes in life still hearing of something I hope that I will be getting peace in my life.

Sometime just live life because everybody not going to be your friend just live and pretend that's just life. Just in world by side have lot friend care about not my family they love me but still not my family go family to gathering that they have but I feel like I'm out of place. But I ask myself why can't I have a family that loves me for what I am? Not what they want me to be. I am strong and wise. Much better but I made it that it wouldn't make me lose my mind, one day my family will see what I did in my life. God showed me favor in my life I know people talk about me behind my back, but I just ask god to help somebody when they are in need don't try to hurt them. I tried to help them, but they talk about me, but I don't care sometimes they cuss me out, call me slow, fat, and ugly, but its ok, I've been call that all my life so I'm used to it, it's just words, it hurts me sometimes and makes me cry to myself in a corner like I did something wrong. That's how my mom treated me all my life, but its ok, people had took from me, told lies to me, but its ok I still live, I didn't finish school but I learned a lot over the year and it made me wise with order. I got help from the Lord because I'm tired of this stuff because if the devil try to attack me in my circumstances because not worthy it just.

CHAPTER 3

Alone in the dark I've never felt so alone the tears stream down my face. I only want to feel you and lie there in my space I sit here in the darkness and I long to hear your voice yet there is nothing.

I can do now prepared you've made your choice my heart will always love you. You'll always be the one. I won't ever forget you. What more could I have done? You used to call me angel and comfort me while I'd cry. That is all I wanted instead I heard goodbye. When you feel you're in the dark there will always be a light, there will always be people who are there for you.

To tell you it's all right when you feel you're all done and isolated on your screen you can find someone to help cause not everyone is mean they can say just anything but not who you are. You know yourself better than them. So their words don't go far, be sure to keep your head up and don't hesitate to smile, it will all get better if you stay here for a while.

I was born in Covington, Georgia my parents Sarah heard and Bennie heard we live in Covington, Georgia in Harris town then my father move to DeKalb County, then it was just me and my sister in Wesley chapel apartment. Then just me, my sister, mom, and father in the two-bedroom apartment, but my mom still beats me with a brace on my leg, then came my little brother we still lived in that apartment as I grow up they were still being mean to me, it got better when I started to go to school, it's better because no one hits me till I bruise.

They started to put me in the slow class so I wasn't walk home from school by myself and more I had transfer school becausedidn't have special education class in there that's why I had transferred school, I started going to Canby Lane Elementary school in DeKalb county, I've seen the war begin as I grew up, I met this man while in high school, my mom was gone then, just me, my sister, and my brother. This time grandma came up here to see what we do because we were young. They placed me in foster care at the time while my mother was in jail, after school my mom bruised me and that's why she went to jail, she beats me even when I did what she said. My grandma from dad's side have my life while at southwest DeKalb high. This man saw me walking home from school and tried to talk to me, but I fell for it, he started bruising me too, when he let me go home to my dad, my dad and mom start looking for me because a younger girl with a grown man they didn't know that well. I fell in love with him but my dad broke that up. Me, sis, and bro started went to the skate ring on Friday night. I and sis started stealing clothes for us to wear, we steal out of stores while dad was at work we were off the chain. Dad went to work, then moved to the candle road apartment up the street from the mall that's where I and my sister go to school. We started hanging out at the mall and steal too. I did a lot of things I'm not pleased with. Then we moved back to Covington Georgia living with my grandma from my dad's side. When watch us didn't work find get too DeKalb county every day my Aunt take me to school DeKalb pick up Marjorie Duncan pick up school been got missed so put in down in Covington I didn't like it we around enoughfamily member when start at my grandma house on my dad side of family that story. On to the story of my adulthood.

Know it in my book put in my book so bear with me you should god for yourself I should put that in no book put in my own words. Now to live in this world honestly people always distract you from doing gods will, even man or husband always got something to say about your god, some say about you but long no god for yourself enough seen matter to you.

All ask god to teach us how to live in this world and not be ashamed in life with what's wrong with the world now because we have wisdom and knowledge at all worried lord. Tired of cry because it hard for me deal with man always got game for you so I tried to be a good women too him tried so hard to do my best to help people but it's not me but its ok I just ask the lord to help me guide others with this book because it ashamed with life I hope one day living good life be happy stop living misery because it is a trip so just be sad and cry out to god to help me.

I didn't have a good childhood and most of my adulthood life because a man treat me like I'm still alone in the dark. I hoped for a way out I sought out gods words when I was little girl. Mom was always mean to me, always shout at me a lot of things, beat me, and make me learn how to take care of myself. I never had a loving mother like everyone else she always shovel me to side. I was picked on in school and in high school I never had anybody like me, I was always alone by myself, nobody talked to me, but my sister then my dad got tired.

Sometimes in life, we leave some stuff alone just live our life because that's just how the world is. Because people going be people who just love them they just care who is hurt, when I went to church try to ask God to forgive this world and to keep coming against me with people. I'm just tired of people calling the police on me like I did something to them, but its ok I read out our daily bread. This story makes sense to me sometimes I get hard feelings for the fact that when people don't like you they talk behind your back, but it's ok I can see my grandchildren. Because my children don't like what I did in life I can't change the past now. I just want my children's hope to be restored. If I were not careful our modern sometimes jaded ears can hear a bit of sarcasm in Jesus question to an invalid do want to get well john 5;6. The obvious would seem to be kidding me, I've been wanting to help for thirty-eight years. I hoped that one day I will conquer something in life without negativity in my life and then the day will come when the risk to remain tight in a bud was more painful than the risk it took to blossom.

    All the years I blamed my mom for mistake in life dealing with the wrong man.
    Tried to keep me a prisoner in my mind, but yet I let them control me like I'm a child but not anymore.
    Lord, lead my way in life because I need to help out in life. I'm still trying to find scriptures to put in my book.
    So bear with me, you all know that the words I put in this book are true.

People always distract you when you try to do Gods will every man or husband always got something to say about you, but long no

God for yourself enough seen matter too you all ask god teacher how live in dis world not be ashamed in life that wrong with world now because we have wisdom and knowledge.

Lord you know alone in world myself with nobody care for me never did always ask myself why I have never been popular in school always pick on by the boys and my family just life when moved Covington Georgia always be with man at night and being gang raped by men because its night. I never had a man to love me for what I am, but its ok Tracey my sister had all man and popular man with car and money never had that because I was the ugly duck in my family. I always had swear makeup hid when I look beautiful to them, I didn't have money to fix myself up, that's why I let myself go because didn't have anyone who likes me like that, so that I cry inside and out because I didn't have it grow, but it's okay, I still had life it has going in but still okay just ask the lord, why me? Why I had to look like that? I just had to look like now I don't feel that way now, I just want to be tiffany, want know friend just like me because what I do just be friend expect what I am but be friend expect what I am but they didn't it ok too just be real too myself I ask lord help me one day beautiful swam live good didn't have pretty face now don't feel that it sad when you been used by people when think your friend is for you are not just tired of try be people please I just want be alone, living my life, doing what I want with my life, I'm just tired of people telling me what to do try make mend with my children that didn't happened so mad with me about this man I am with me about this man I am with but I'm a little sad about it now time me live for me not nobody else might had leave that man be with my children and grandchildren I am tired been a slave for people doing what they say, because they're old. Go with the life stop holding me back it lot got do with my life so help me please because I need a change in my life lord from the people not get in better with it I want to do my dream and finish write my book.

Always take stay with grandparent with my cousin they live there to but state put my sister with grandparent because they thought it was safe to stay with my mom. Still, when they stay with her mom and dad, grandma always clean up or wash the dishes. If you don't do what grandma and granddad say you get a whooping, just stay down in Jamestown, I like being with my dad's mom because I had freedom there with her, because I was being treated like how a child is supposed to be, my mom's grandma didn't like to play with the boys and go out the yard my aunt and I had there cool the where my mom's sister there was cool they taught how to dance and everything over a year grandma got killed in a carwreck when she was gone my other grandma started to get sick so I was by myself again, because they were gone from my life hear come my dad get sick then he were gone didn't know family member but my aunt on my mom's side of the family they were the only one in my life after grownup, then start have children too didn't raise them either but I wish now should raise my children better with life I met Mr. and Mrs. Sims and Rence fisher they became family too and my children they help us out took us place I just do own thing now wish stay with pastors Sims and Rence fisher because been my life when I going through this tough time in life now older I got still look for god to change my lifestyle because it was terrible when I grownup, but it's still not the same I just wanted a normal lifestyle, to have a husband and be happy with my life, but it just can't do that always try get people understand me, because I'm nobody ok just want to be person like everybody else want be success just live vacation life, have a nice house and be comfort with it hope be living that again with money when I want go vacation just go not be hidden from it because I want to live life to the fullest.

CHAPTER 4

I wish I weren't alone. Once when I was little I was happy and carefree I used to run around laughing until it was time for tea, I used to play games and smile all the time, I used to feel on top of the world, I used to feel time, it was amazing how thing change when people let you down and how that once happy face turn into a solemn frown, you search for someone who cares, anyone who's understanding, anyone who dare loneliness, it hurts, it kills you deep inside, it make you feel empty, it stop you in your stride, you cry yourself to sleep hugging your pillow tight, wishing for someone who cares, anyone who dares the loneliness it hurt it kill you deep inside it make you feel empty it stop you in your stride you cry yourself to sleep hugging your pillow tight wishing for someone to hold You through the night one when I was little I was happy and carefree now my life full of sadness, pain, and mystery once when I was little I was never on my own but now I pray at night I wish I weren't alone.

Say do even when was child so each day I learned how take control of my life always ask god why your me when people do both harm to me why me lord why me I have suck bad life when I grownup. When you're alone in life don't have nobody to talk to, or be friend with you, it's sad, but you have to keep going, just living and finally find friends, they are alcohol and drugs and then one of them then now come personality change because street got you den then experience all kind lifestyle situation then hear go jail mental health placebecause can't get together then got called slow all type name called them you got worried folk in world just care about people just one of them when life past you by start think like people in street act like them to because you have no know body in life to guide you right way that parent if raise children raise right when they don't go wrong way if you don't raise your children if raise going be mess up like tiffany were been raise from street be your friend they are not that world is mess up with foolish people in it I know I did a lot of stuff one please to God, but in got pay for mistake that pastor been say it process in your life why that because if don't know Christ for self be lost then try find way in life in dis world sometime you just tired stuff people do to you hope one day I will be success in life I just want to live normal life be happy I stayout drama and stress so just tired I hope that people seek good in me not bad my children don't have enough with me because I put man for them my mom said I am real not in her marriage she beat me so bad it just anybody mess it ok just worlds I am still seek god will do it will to death put want on career when I say did something in my life I keep pressing through it, because it gets hard when everybody turn their back on you. I hope and pray that get breakthrough in my book confused in this world, its ok to still hold on to my words and Gods words, but get hard, but I so try to just tired sometime in life stillhearing of something I hope that I getting peace in my life.

When I didn't have anything to wear I go two boys in rain when my mom put of pay her rent sleep in her living room but it were ok because didn't have nobody my mom had a small apartment with one of my child and my sisters children stay there too, but we like shit it okay to but I tried my best to keep it together, but it wasn't proper at all me and my boy used to sit at the library when it gets dark we didn't have anywhere to go it was sad. Because it was a trip, because when trying to deal with shy family members do you I cry lot time as if it was ok just life, but I find a way to make life easy for me and my boy, but it's okay just still went on with life thendidn't have no help, I lost everything to my storage, I was renting, but its ok just life, but I will find a way to make life easy for me and my boys but it ok just life still went on with life then start get apartment try to live a clean life that didn't happened, I start deal with baby daddy and other friends, it was a struggle ,but its ok when church people feel sorry for us brought us car ride with his women it been a struggle all my life now, it then start get on apartment try live clean life that didn't happened I start get on apartment try live clean life that didn't daddy and other friend it were struggled but it ok when church people feel sorry for brought.

Lord you know I'm alone in this world, I am by myself with nobody to care for me and my family, I don't care about me they never did always ask myself why never been popular in school pick body and family just life whenmoved Covington Georgia always be with man at night and been gang rape by men because its ok for me for what I am but it ok Tracey sister had all man and popular man with car and money never had that because I was the ugly duck in the family I always had swear makeup hide when I look beautiful to them. I didn't have money to fix myself go ,because I didn't have anyone I like so that I cry inside and out because I didn't have it grow but it okay still had life it has going in but it okay still had okay just ask lords why me why I had just ask lords why me why I had look like that just had no pretty face at all, but its ok just want be like now don't feel that way now just be tiffany want know friend just like me because what I am but they didn't it ok too just be real to myself I ask the lord to help me one day a beautiful swim and live a goodlife.

Say do even when was child so each day I learned how take control of my life always ask god why your me when people do both harm to me why me lord why me I have suck bad life when I grownup when you alone in life don't have nobody talk on be friend with you it sad but you have kept going just living finally find friend they are alcohol and drug and then one of them then now come personality change because street got you den then experience all kind lifestyle situation then hear go jail mental health placebecause can't get together then got called slow all type name called them you got worried folk in world just care about people just one of them when life past you by start think like people in street act like them to because you have no know body in life to guide you right way that parent if raise children raise right when they don't go wrong way if you don't raise your children if raise going be mess up like tiffany were been raise from street be your friend they are not that world is mess up with foolish people in it I know didlot stuff one please to god but in got pay for mistake that pastor been say it process in your life why that because if don't know Christ for self be lost then try find way in life in dis world sometime you just tired stuff people do to you hope one day I will be success in life I just want to live normal life be happy I stay out drama and stress so just tired I hope that people seek good in me not bad my children don't have enough with me because I put man for them my mom said I am real not in her marriage she beat me so bad it just anybody mess it ok just worlds I am still seek god will do it will to death put want on career when I say did something in my life I keep pressed through it because it get hardwhen everybody turn back on you I hope pray that get breakthrough in my book confused in dis world itok too still hold on to my words and god words but get hard but I so try to just tired sometime in life stillhearing of something I hope that I getting peace in my life.

My children life they turn around dis grace my name all I can say is lordhelp me then try escape thing in my life it seen want go away tired of runfrom people not going support me what I want to do tired set boundary inmy life that don't work tired people hinder me been ask lord help me in race sometime sit watch other people be popular the me I'm got grownup start have children that couldn't raise because didn't have money and a house to put them in. Stay with my grandma when they were little didn't know who dad were some of them I were young then put didn't know them, but I didn't kill them, I gave them to family members to take care of them when I was young then at the time I didn't have a normal childhood, I didn't grownup in a perfect family, but I made it through life, I got with the wrong crowds, I started to get in trouble and do drugs, but I'm not the shame. My experience life all my life I had dodge people because so where lock room or lockout because just leave me alone didn't have nobody to talk or play with young lady because so where lock room on porches to dad get home didn't have what sister bother had taken and run with it.

Lord I need a place for myself to get out and around people that drink tell lie on that help because I feel like that use all the year by same man because just not fair at all tired help people it ok but alight to so I need get waves for wild be myself and living because just too much people don't treating you same treat on yourself sometime in life back way from thing, its ok I just need space to breathe it in, so don't live like you're in a prison, everything you say don't matter to him, I need to get away from him from him for wild see how living without man because I tried so hard with dis but it ok my family want help me at all because it sad don't have known for here to go need help lords lord help me because I'm tired of this stuff because it devil try attack me I ask is to you please help me all in my circumstance because not worthy it just want finish my book and live my life to fullness do god will tired of cry with mess in shield me because have good heart I need stop let people mistreat me call me slow and crazy it ok just tired of stuff because it too late try find my life in god work keep me with keep me with sound mind devil at me want me to break but I won't let the devil step in. Because it won't be fair, I'm not declaring victory over my life it want be fair to me god, I hope I will be successful in life, I hope one day I will be successful in life, I hope one day because I want to stop worrying about what people think, I just want a better life for myself because it going get better with it people want me look stupid but I'm not.

WALK IN MY SHOES

If you walked in my shoes for a day.
You'd know how I love you in suck a way.
You'd share the aching my heart for every.
Moment we spent apart you'd feel electricity.
When I touch your skin and the warmth;
I received from seeing you grin.
You'd see me tumble into your eyes how they brighten.
Up the greyest skies you'd smell the sweetness;
of your aura radiating like fresh picked flora.
You'd hear bow saying three simple words is.
Like hearing the sweetest song or birds.
If you walked in my shoes for the rest of your life.
You'd know that I'm thankful that you're myself.

CHAPTER 5

Isolated on your screen.

Candle when I'm out to wonder and roam so no matter how far

I am I may always return home.

Isolated on your screen when you feel you're in the dark there will always be light.

There are people whoare there for you

To tell you it's alright when you feel you're all alone

Isolated on your screen you can find someone to help.

Because not everyone is mean.

They can say just anything but not who you are you know yourself better than them

So their words don't go far be sure to keep your head up and don't hesitate to smile

It will all get better if you stay here for a while.

All of my life I was living in lie it seem thatmy childhood flown.

Right by my daddy walked out and I had to stay strong so my spirit wouldn't die.

Now I've grownup too fast trying to make this life lost

I pushed to move forward but I'm struck in my past

tell me what girl to do forget about it through that not something I can do

What done is done isn't that truth

Part of me died when I was child and my adulthood too

I had five children didn't none of them because I want man care about at all I they want what can do them I they want what can do them but tired of help them with everything because didn't make no sense always why me?

Why can just live my own life for change?

I alone be broken in my life then tired be in when you feel you're in the dark

There are will anything but not who you are you know yourself better than them

So their words don't go far be sure to keep your head up and don't hesitate to smile

It will all get better if you stay here for a while

My children life they turn around dis grace my name all I can say is lordhelp me then try escape thing in my life it seen want go away tired of run from people not going support me what I want to do tired set boundary inmy life that don't work tired people hinder me been ask lord help me in race sometime sit watch other people be popular the me I'm got grownup start have children that couldn't raise because didn't have money and a house to put them in stay with my grandma when they were little didn't know who dad were some of them I were young then put didn't know them, but didn't kill them i gave them to family me member take care of them I were young then at time didn't have normal children life didn't grownup home perfect family but I made it through life got with wrong crowd start get in trouble do drug but I not shame just experience life all my life I had dodge people because so where lock room or lockout because just leave me alone didn't have nobody to talk or play with young lady because so where lock room on porches to dad get home didn't have what sister bother had taken and run with it.

Know how feel be lock out door can't get in house to my dad come home. Then your mom beat on me half death what can I say just child my mom broken Up lot of my toy and clothes that my grandma brought me be mistreat by man and use me but it ok think god law thing happened me in my life it ok think god law thing happenedme in my life it ok still live still seek god words I hope pray that god give me breakthrough in my life may be one day I will be success in life I am tired of junk I had go through with man lords bless me with own house that I call home that all ask for seek your king that get that call tiffany house when keep get out people tell get out lord step in for me please all ask help me get my own becauseI am tired been put outdoor all the year been blame my mom for mistake in life deal with wrong man try keep me in prison in mind but yet let them control me like I'm let child but not so lords lead my way in life because I'm help out in life still try find scripture put in my book so bear with me youshould god for yourself I should put that in no book for you read you all know it in my book put in my own worlds how to live in this worlds honestly people always distract you what try to do god will even man or husband always got some to say about you but long no god for yourself enough seen matterto you all ask god teacher how live in dis worlds not be ashamed in life that wrong with worlds now because we have wisdom and knowledge at all worried.

When I didn't have anything to wear I go two boys in rain when my mom put of pay her rent sleep in her living room but it were ok because didn't have nobody my mom had a small apartment with one of my child and my sisters children stay there too, but we like shit it okay to but I tried my best to keep it together, but it wasn't proper at all me and my boy used to sit at the library when it gets dark we didn't have anywhere to go it was sad. Because it was a trip, because when trying to deal with shy family members do you I cry lot time as if it was ok just life, but I find a way to make life easy for me and my boy, but it's okay just still went on with life then didn't have no help, I lost everything to my storage, I was renting, but its ok just life, but I will find a way to make life easy for me and my boys but it ok just life still went on with life then start get apartment try to live a clean life that didn't happened, I start deal with baby daddy and other friends, it was a struggle ,but its ok when church people feel sorry for us brought us car ride with his women it been a struggle all my life now, it then start get on apartment try live clean life that didn't happened I start get on apartment try live clean life that didn't daddy and other friend it were struggled but it ok when church people feel sorry for brought.

Sometime in life just wonder happened when I was a kid why was I mistreated so much why I want love other children were why? Be battle while been child and grown up lords when year went by still doingwhat people tell me just I were enough because just didn't have no body talk for me.

Even when I child so each day I learned how take control of my life always ask god why me when people do both harm to me why me lord? Ask why me? I had suck bad life style when I grownup when you alone in life don't have nobody talk on be friend with you it sad but you have kept going justliving finally find friend they are alcohol and drug and then one of them then now come personality change because street got you den then experience all kind lifestyle situation then hear go jail mental health place because can't get together then got called slow all type name called them you got weird folk in worlds just care about people just one of them I'm got grownup start have children that couldn't raise because didn't have money and house put them in stay with my grandma when they were little didn't knowwho dad were some of them .but I didn't kill of them I gave them to family member take care of them I were young at time didn't know how raise a children but all say done that still love them just could do it because didn't have normal children life didn't grownup home perfect family but I made it through life got with wrong crowd start get in trouble do drug but I not shame just experience life all my life I had dodge people because just leaves me alone didn't have nobody to talk or play with younglady because so where lock room or locked outdoor porch to dad get home didn't have what my sister bother had taken run with it.

CHAPTER 6

CHANGE THE WAY I THINK

I ask god change me because it hurt insides change mind of thing

Is not true be try but don't work all time. I cried out to lords to help me what are your thoughts? Be anything envy people mad with words, what would you do when you're alone in the dark with yourself I had a dream that can't do when I can be success to it I hope one day can pursue it because people always wait around 24 hours a day. How would I do that lords want finish my book when I can be success in life been writer want tell my story to public let know been through it that why I am write this book let know this long journey or race with worlds against devil spiritually thing you try handle thing with old worlds but get rough I keep push god words because people do things that make you mad with them.

Sometime just live life because everybody not going be friend just live pretendthat just life. Just in world by side have lot friend care about not my family theylove me but still not my family go family to gathering that they have but I feel like out place .but I ask myself why can have family like that love me for what I am not what want to be I am strong and wise much better but I made it wouldn't made it lose my mind one day my family see good what I did in my life. God showed me favored in my life I know people talk about me behind my back just ask god help somebodywhen they I need don't be tried hurt them I tried help them but they say talk about them, but I don't sometime cuss me out call me slow, fat, ugly, but its ok I've been call that all my life but I use to it just worlds be hurt me sometime I cry too myself like in corner like did some wrong that how my mom treating me over be treat all my life but it ok people had took from me toldlie on me but it ok still live I didn't finish school but I learned a lot over the year than make it I got wiser the older I got lord help me because I'm tired of this stuff because it devil try attack me all in my circumstance because not worthy it just.

Lord help me because I'm tired of this stuff because it devil try attack me. I ask is too you please help me all in circumstance because not worthy it just want finish my book and live my life too fullness do god will tired of cry with mess in shield me because I have a good heart I need stop let people mistreat me call me slow and crazy it ok just tired of stuff because it too late try find my life my life in god words keep me with sound mind devil at me want me to break but I'm not lord I am declaration victory over my life not let devil step in because it want be fair to me god I hope I will day will be success in life because stop worry about what people think just want better life for myself because it going get better with it people want me look stupid but I'm not all my life want own house nice car and swim pool in my back they all dream but hope that God will reveal all my dreams and talk to myself about the thing I tired of struggle with my life.

I want everything, I want a trip, explore the world, it ok but I wished try hard get my published when I can living good life when I were child and since been grownup I hope that give full blessing too me I hope prayer that receive it because I did reserve better in life I hope one day be send my book too prison for lady in there show then long journal of process but seek Gods will, it will let God bless you too.

Always take stay with grandparent with my cousin they live there to but state put my sister with grandparent because they thought it was safe to stay with my mom. Still, when they stay with her mom and dad, grandma always clean up or wash the dishes. If you don't do what grandma and granddad say you get a whooping, just stay down in Jamestown, I like being with my dad's mom because I had freedom there with her, because I was being treated like how a child is supposed to be, my mom's grandma didn't like to play with the boys and go out the yard my aunt and I had there cool the where my mom's sister there was cool they taught how to dance and everything over a year grandma got killed in a car wreck when she was gone my other grandma started to get sick so I was by myself again, because they were gone from my life hear come my dad get sick then he were gone didn't know family member but my aunt on my mom's side of the family they were the only one in my life after grownup, then start have children too didn't raise them either but I wish now should raise my children better with life I met Mr. and Mrs. Sims and Rence fisher they became family too and my children they help us out took us place I just do own thing now wish stay with pastors Sims and Rence fisher because been my life when I going through this tough time in life now older I got still look for god to change my lifestyle because it was terrible when I grownup, but it's still not the same I just wanted a normal lifestyle, to have a husband and be happy with my life, but it just can't do that always try get people understand me, because I'm nobody ok just want to be person like everybody else want be success just live vacation life, have a nice house and be comfort with it hope be living that again with money when I want go vacation just go not be hidden from it because I want to live life to the fullest.

When I didn't have anything to wear I go two boys in rain when my mom put of pay her rent sleep in her living room but it were ok because didn't have nobody my mom had a small apartment with one of my child and my sisters children stay there too, but we like shit it okay to but I tried my best to keep it together, but it wasn't proper at all me and my boy used to sit at the library when it gets dark we didn't have anywhere to go it was sad. Because it was a trip, because when trying to deal with shy family members do you I cry lot time as if it was ok just life, but I find a way to make life easy for me and my boy, but it's okay just still went on with life then didn't have no help, I lost everything to my storage, I was renting, but its ok just life, but I will find a way to make life easy for me and my boys but it ok just life still went on with life then start get apartment try to live a clean life that didn't happened, I start deal with baby daddy and other friends, it was a struggle ,but its ok when church people feel sorry for us brought us car ride with his women it been a struggle all my life now, it then start get on apartment try live clean life that didn't happened I start get on apartment try live clean life that didn't daddy and other friend it were struggled but it ok when church people feel sorry for brought.

i

CHAPTER 7

THE SHELL

I know so many people.
But do they know me?
They recognize the face but that all they ever see.
They see the shell they think is me but they don't.
See the stuff insides the thing that are buried the thing.
I try to hide there are thing under the makeup clothes and the.
And the style there are secret hidden under that big phony smile.
Inside my heart is thunder storm like storm and if I were to break.
It come pouring like a swam I dwell where it dark wet and cold and
I think many thoughts that nobody know then there that one person who
In my soul can shine a light and discover all sins hidden in my eyes
He comfort he caution and I say don't tell he is the one who know me
The me under the shell.

And when living Covington Georgia going down there around Cuzco start deal with grown man by walk street Covington been fast little girl dad still live in Atlanta at time when me and sister and bro in Covington Georgia still going Atlanta see my dad been with going too mall he where stay with uncle on five point train station still going have with my friend on weekend go home Sunday at my grandma house with all my aunt where at my grandma house my still gone out picture then my dad start get sickover year my grandma start get sick over year it were my world just over with start have children young age it got worst didn't want.

No kids because my mom didn't me young start have leave them going behind them kids just leave them with family member but it ok too but now I got older now learning cause little different my kids I can't change.

Past be better people in father that I met William Johnson house program,he is older guy be taught me what is life is he know been mistreat in my life he start take care of me when didn't have no family. Griffin Georgia William I stay same apartment comply William my bad bone every sense I meet him William I living together now he's like a husband to me, treats me like how a woman is supposed to be been William going 11 year now still live in same house now he help with me didn't have enough he was enough. He never left me because I didn't have any money, people kept telling him to leave me because I were broken but he didn't now live in house that rent we have to Car in drive we had bless but still together even I'm writing my book.

Say do even when was child so each day I learning how take control of my life always ask god why me when people do both harm too me why me lord why me I have suck bad life I grownup when you alone in life don't have nobody talk are be friend with you it sad but you have kept going just living finally find friend they are alcohol and drug and then one of them then now come personality change because street got you den then experience all kind lifestyle situation then hear go jail mental health place because can't get together then got called slow all type name called them you got weird folk in world just care about people just one of them when life past you by start think like people in street act like them too because you have no know body in life too guideyou right way that parent if you raise children raise right when they don't go wrong way if you don't raiseyour children wrong way going be mess up like tiffany were been raise from street experience all kind thing it very important that you should go choice in life because think street be your friend they are not that world is mess up with foolish people in it I know did lot are not that world is messed up with foolish people in it I know did lot stuff one please too god but I got pay for mistaken that pastors been say it process in your life why that because if don't know Christ for self be lost then try find way in life this worlds.

But the pain you forget too appreciate love if you haven't seen. The hate ill you forget the meaning of smile and laughter and your heart is left abate. I have known the strength and courage it require too get it right to face the thing that holed you down and hold your head up and fight before I was someone I didn't want to bet then start get on apartment try live clean life that didn't happened I start deal with baby daddy and other friend it were struggled but it ok when church people feel sorry for us brought us a car get around it then my daddy when tore it up ride with his women it been in struggled all my life now it time stop hear am run from baby daddy and low with myself and children I got in trouble with law with myself and children it ok too just life then try find boyfriend love me still use me for my body I have gang rape too when I grownup by man lonely see at night but ok too all my life people took from me living in my house didn't pay me enough but it ok too just tired living my life like that I hope one day get break don't want let keep happened to me I hope pray god step in and the verse of that sweet old song it flutter and murmurs still a girl will is the wind will and thought of youth are long thought I remember the gleam and glooms that dart across the school girls brain the song and silence in the heart that in part are prophecies and in part are long wild and vain the voice of that and the voice of that fistful song on and is never still a girl will is the wind will and the thought of youth are long thought there are thing of which I may not speak there are dream that cannot die there are thought that make the strong heart weak and bring a mist before the eye and the words of that fatal song come over me like a chill a girl will is the winds and the thought of youth are long thought strange to me now are the forms I meet when I visited the dear old town but the native air is pure and sweet and tree that covers shadows each well-known street as they balance up and down are singing the beautiful song are sighting and whispering still a girl will is the winds will and the thought of youth are long thought and deer words are fresh and fair and with joy that is almost pain my heart goes back to wander there and among the dream, of the days that were I find my lost youth again and the strange and beautiful song the groves are repeating it still a girl will is the wind s will and thought of youth are long thought write in book all the words that I have spoken to you lord instruction Jeremiah 30;2 this caught my attention recently because writing is such as integral part of my devotional life documented

In journal while the circumstance

And context of god instruction too Jeremiah are very different from our experience with god writing in a book is helpful tool for bolstering our devotion lives journaling forces me too linger over a verse longer that I normally would during my devotions if a particular verse phrase catch e my eye I write it down and begin meditating on it resting through Jeremiah recently this phrase jumped out of me their ears are uncircumcised they cannot Listen Jer 6;10 as I wrote this phrase I pondered what it that are covered blocked un able to hear god voice as I wrote out the passage I remember that circumcised is also described in god words as a sign of spiritual rebirth roman 2;29 god covenant genesis 17;11 and spiritual humility Deuteronomy 10;16 I was remind of some key spiritual truth I had not considered in a Longtime circumcise my ear so I can hear you Warning. Your instruct your encouragement and your assurance the concept of circumcised ear become more mean meaningful when I incorporated it into my prayer suddenly a passage that seemed only about the history of rebellious Israel had a very practical personal application journaling also prepare me for a triall experience while serve lord in Asia.

Sometime just live life because everybody not going be friend just live pretend that just life just in world by side have lot friend care about not my family they love me but still not my family go family gathering that they have but I feel like out place but I ask myself why can have family like that love me for what I am not want to be I am strong and wise much better but I made it wouldn't made it lose my mind one day my family see good what I did in my life. God on show me favored in my life god on show me favored in my life I know people talk about me behind my back just ask god help somebody when they I need don't be tired hurt them I tried help them but they say talk about them but I don't sometime cuss me out call me slow fat ugly but it ok been call that all my life but I use to it just word be hurt me sometimes I sit and cry to myself like in comer like did some wrong that how my mom treating me over year so use on it so know that how we treat all my life but it ok people had took from me told lie on me had took from me told lie on me but it ok still like I didn't finish school but I learning over year than make it I got wise with older I got.

Because think treat be your friend they are not that world is mess up with foolish. People in it I know did lot stuff one please too god but I got pay for mistake that pastors been say it.

Process in your life why that because if don't know Christ for self be lost then try find way in life this world that why try tell people this world avoid around you because it good not nobody that why you

Have keep god in your pocket and try living right because this world isn't promise to you everybody sayin generally that not going church because preach out pocket or just want money but just stupid just life I hope one day we learn how read bible make good choice in life don't get too old when you can't turn around it like pastor say got have mindset if you don't you might be in bad shaped but always forgive.

Me because I'm human in this world and it promise to you everybody say in generally that not going church because preacher out pocket or just want money but just stupid just life I hope one day we learn how read bible make good choice in life don't get too old when you can't turn around it like pastors say got have mindset if you don't you might be bad shaped always forgive me, because I'm human in this world people in world just can't get right that why all say it my family want help me because learn live for yourself not people not hold hand always people always look some free hand out wonder why life so darn fine can't handle it all the year been blamed on my mom for mistake in life deal with wrong man try keep in prison in mind but yet let them take control over my life I'm a child but not so lord lead my way in life because I'm help out in life still try find scriptures put in my book for you read you all some people just don't want see do good with your life always tried knock you down about anything you do it so hard living with some body, try pursue your dream I'm always negative to say about hope, but God giving little faith go on if hard be homeless in my life because want peace in it lord just ask give me finish this book when living better life be in with myself lord I ask help me with journey on please this man argue every day about this book why I can write a book about my life be support too, it lords why been ask you lord about open door for me because always say don't pay no bill at but I doing just pay car notes try pay off that pay on bill when I living enjoyed life and be happy so lord want be happy in not misery because it just crazy just because write a book.

CHAPTER 8

WHY?

Why do you tear me down when all I do is build you up?
Why do hate me so much?
Why do you deny my touch is drinking that important and family?
So expendable you call me names and tell me I'm the one blame
It's all my fault.
I deserve a verbal assault not a bruise on mybody only scare on my soul
I am alone.
I am scared I'd be better on my own what happened
To the love we shared, I am fat, a slut, a whore, a liar when
All I am crier you say I'm not faithful but it's our relationship that not stable
I don't deserve this I am a good person let's try a kiss to release my burden
When will you stop the drunken argument that mean nothing I am tired,
I am worn out, I can't go on, knowing I am.
Nobody knows that the empty the smile
I wear isn't the real one.
It was left behind in the past because
I left you there nobody known I am laughing I wish

you were here.
　　Nobody knows how painful it is, stay strong they say, they think that I am strong They say it won't kill me but I you.
　　They think I am free, but I feel mystery.
　　Nobody knows I need you,
　　They think I can do it on my own but they don't know.

They don't know I am crying when I am alone, the hardest thing I ever did was to let go of you and look forward instead of back at the past, I wonder how long this broken heart will last I guess everything you said was a lie, so I'm going to move forward or at least I'm going to try how many times can a heart break before it shuttles or does it even matter?

I've sat and cried over you way too much, just wishing one more time I could feel your touch, but you don't care and neither should I, so I'm going to move on or at least I'm going to try all of my life.

I was living a lie it seen that my childhood has flood right by my daddy walked out and I had nowhere to cry I had to stay strong so my spirit wouldn't die now.

I've grownup too fast trying to make this life last I pushed to move forward but I'm stuck in my past tell me what's a girl to do? Forget about it through and through that's not something I can do, what's done is done isn't that the truth?

Even when I was a child, each day I learned how take control of my life, to always ask god why me when People do harm to me, why me lord? Why me? I have such a bad life growing up.

When you're alone in life and don't have anybody to talk or be friends with, you would be sad, but you have to keep going, just living, until you finally find friends they are alcohol and drugs and one of them now come with personality changes because street got you, then experience all kind lifestyle situation then hear go jail mental health place because can't get together then got called slow all type name called them you got called slow all type called them you weird folk in the world just care about people just one of them.

When life past you by, you start thinking like people in the streets act like them too because you have no body in life to guide you through the right way to be a Parent. If you raise children, raise them right so they don't go the wrong way, so they won't be messed up like tiffany, she has been raised from the street and experienced all kinds of things. It is very important that you should go choice in life because think street be your friend they are not that world is mess up with foolish people in it.

I know I did a lot of stuff, one please in it I know did lot stuff one please too God, but I got to pay for my mistakes. That's what the pastor said. It's a process in your life. Why is that? If you don't know it's because Christ foe self be lost then try find way in life in this world. That's why try tell people this world avoid around you because it good not nobody that why you have keep god in your pocket and try living right because dis world isn't promise too you Everybody say in generally pocket or just life I hope one day we learned how read bible make good choice in life don't get too old when you can't turn around it like pastor say got have mindset if you Don't you might be bad shape always forgive me because I'm human in dis worlds just can't get right that Why All Say It My Fam Ilywant Help Me Because Learn Live For Yourself Not People Not Hold Hand Always People Always Look Some Free Hand Out Wonder Why Life So Damm Fire Cant Handle It All The Year Been Blame My Mom For Mistake In Life Deal With Wrong Man Try Keep Me In Prison In Mind But Yet Let Them Control Me Like Im Child But Not So Lord Lead My Way In Life Because Im Help Out In Life Still Try To Find Scripture To Put In My Book For All Of You To Read.

Before I became strong I knew what it was too weak. How difficult it was to love yourself, to find the wholeness that you seek. Before I knew the light, I have had my fair share of darkness too. Where my world falls into a hopelessness and I didn't know how to get through it, for I have known the tear it takes, the courage to stand up again when you are broken down and bruised, and you know nothing but the pain you forget to appreciate love if you haven't seen the hate you'll forget the meaning of a smile and laughter and your heart is left abate. I have known the strength and courage it requires to get it right, to face the thing that held you down and hold your head up, and hold your head up and fight before I was someone I didn't want to be, I was lost battered and defeated before I knew how to be me?

Do not copy the behavior and custom of the world but let god transform you into a new person by changing the way you think then you will learn to know god has not given us a spirit of god has not given us a spirit of fear and timidity but fear but of power, love, self-disciple 2 TIM 1;7 but fear and distrust of life and people isn't from god yet it seemed hard wired into our mind were afraid at being love always 7 weapon to conquer your spiritual enemies number 25;18 the whole armor EPH 6;12 6;14 EPH 6;10 for we do not wrestle against flesh and blood but against principalities finally my breathe be strong in the lord and in the power of his might this verse indicates the armors of god is for the blood bought EPHE 6;15 6;14 put on the helmet genesis 2;25 the breastplate genesis 3;7 the belt the shoes ps37;23 the sword the shield EPH 6;15 praying in the spirit EPH 6;18 6;13 the whole armor of god roman 12;14;21 Joshua 10;6 Joshua 1;9 dealing with enemies put principles before personalities proverb 11;3 roman2;11 PS 25;21 2king 5;16 like 10;19 proverb 14;12 Joshua 1 PSL 19-105 matt 4-10 the lord will grant that the enemies who rise up against you will be defeated before they will come at your direction but flee from you in seven DEUT 28;7 no weapon forged against you will prevail and you will refute every tongue that accuses you this is this is vindication from me declare the lords Isiah 54;17 the integrity of the upright guide them but the unfaithful are destroyed by their vindication from me declare the lords Isiah 54;17 the integrity of the upright guides them but the unfaithful are destroyed by their duplicity proverb 11;3 my life all of my life I was living in a lie it seen that my childhood has flown right by my daddy walked out and I had nowhere to cry I had to stay strong so my spirit wouldn't die now I've grownup too fast trying to make this life last I push to move forward but I'm stuck in my past tell me what a girl too do ?

Forget about it thought and through that not something I can do what done is done aunt that the truth light up the ways of illuminated the blocked road with the brightest spark light up my mind when I'm feeling low help me keep the dark thought away and make my mind glow light up my worlds with you. Away everything that is evil, everything that is scary and vile, light up my life.

> I am tired of struggle
> Now it time lord with confused
> And struggle in life so now wait on god blessing me financial so don't

Ask anyone enough because get stress to me. Not people look at you some. Type way now when you got enough it sad because all want you some money.

It sad because just got enough can't pay off my car because just don't have no money I tried to suit my goal because it's sad people always look down on me. I hope one day I will achieve my goal because I need it. I pray lord will give high favor blessings on my Book because I need it. I'm tired of the struggle with money issued because it's not worth it.

I am sorry about life because it's sad to me because it's ok I had struggled my whole life because I can't buy clothes or shoes, lord I need a place for myself too. God, get out around people that drinks, tell lies on that help because I feel like that they use me all the time. I'm tried it's not fair at all by same man it ok, but it's alright to be wild, to be myself, and living because it's just too much People don't treat you the same as you treat yourself. Sometimes in life back way from thing its Ok I just need a place to breathe in. it so don't living like in prison everything say don't Matter to him I need get away from him for wild see how living without man because Its sad tried so hard with dis but it ok my family want help me at all because it sad don't have nowhere to go, I need help lord.

CHAPTER 9

Change is All

No one will ever know how I feel.
I cannot even explain it.
Nobody to love. Nobody to blame.
Everyone is always the same, nothing to care about. No reason to lie for I'm me, myself, and I.
No one sees what I see. Nobody left to care for me.
It's kind of sad knowing what true cause then you know who is there for you.
Most of them just put on that act. A lot of them talk bad about me behind my back.
Thanks for making me feel this way, there's nothing more I should have to say.
All the time I was alone, makes me feel weird when someone's home has no family for support.
No friend or people to care, I wonder why I didn't go anywhere every night.
Crying myself to sleep some time.
I wish someone loved me, no hope, no Love, no life, no friend.
The pain never ends sometime I ask what did I do to deserve this, but nobody answers me saying there is no good to remember.
I always yell at myself asking why me why I'm sitting in an empty spare room, no one talk about how I feel, no one ask me what I feel, is anyone out there in this harsh

world we live in?

    Sometimes I begin to wonder, sometimes I'm harsh on myself morning come and I wake up wishing I was never born please help others because today lives are being taken out of this world just as easy as they are coming in you can change this tough world.

    Ripped pants broken heart

I live my life, I tried my best to follow all my dreams, my great endeavors were forever bursting at The seams and though I tried to love what/s mine I failed and I confess to my bones and knee made pants.

Like these suffer much distress I heard a tearing sound and I thought it was my heart when I looked down and frown at my pants, they fell apart the ripped sound was not around at the greatest time for when my knee

Skin felt cold air it was less than sublime and now I live my life knee and now I I've my life knee bare against the world alone now everyone can plainly see my pale skin joint and bone my ripped up pant like Frankenstein I may just sew together or perhaps make my pant short to wear in warmer weather my pant are done I have moved on they've done their master well and pant don't live forever not as far as I can tell but there one problem I can't solve and it I truly hate does one bury their old dead pants or do they just cremate and the verse of that sweet old song it flutter and murmurs still a girl will is the wind will and thought of youth are long though I remember the gleams and glooms that dart across the school girl brain the song and the silence in heart that in part are prophecies and in part are long wild and vain and the voice of that and the voice of that fitful song sing on and is never still a girl will is wind will and the thought there are thing of which I may not speak there are dream that cannot die there are thoughts that make the strong heart weak and bring a pallor into the creek and a mist before the eye and the words of that fatal song come over me like a chill a girl will is the winds will and the thought of youth are long though strange to me now are the forms I meet when I visit the dear old town but the native air is pure and sweet and tree that they balance up and down are singing the beautiful song are sighing and whispering still a girl will is the winds will and the thought of youth are long though and deeming wood are fresh and fair and with joy that is almost pain my heart goes back to wander there and among the dream of the days that were I find my lost youth again and the strangle and beautiful song the groves are repeating it still a girl will is the wind will and thought of youth are long though tired I'm tired listening to the sound of my tear, tired of constantly battling my fears, tired of struggling with challenges that continuously reappear, I'm tired of wasting my days submersed in despair, tried of words piercing my heart like sharp spears, tired of living a life that is one big blur, I'm tired of pretending while deep insides I cared, tired of being stuck in toxic relationships and atmospheres tired of hypocrisy and lie in a world full of fakes and veneers I'm tired of trying to believe, I'm tried of battled defeat just tried of feeling this way can I be spare.

Know it in my book put in my book so bear

With me you should god for yourself I should put that in no book for you read you all know it in my book put in my own word now. Too live in dis world honestly people always distract you what try to do

God will even man or husband always got some to say about you got some to say about you but long no god

Too you all ask god teacher how live this world not be ashamed in life that wrong with world now because we have wisdom and knowledge at All worried lord tried of cry because it hard for me deal with man always got game for You so i tried be a good women too him tired so hard do best help people but it not me but it ok just ask lord help me guide with dis book because it ashamed with life I hope.

One day living good life be happy stop living misery because it is trip so just sad and cry childhood and most of my adulthood life because had man treat me.

So still in alone in dark when i was little girl mom always was mean to me always shout out of lot thing beat me make me learning how take care of myself never had.

Mom love like everyone else she always shavel me too side i wear pickon in school and high school never had nobody too like me always alonwe by myself nobody too like me always alone by myself nobody talk but my sister then my dad got tired

Or yourself enough seen matter

I need to move on says my head I need to decide says my mind I envy her I envy the fact you don't understand what this feel like at all I want hurt you I want to be with you I want to be with you.

I want hurt you I want to be with you I want this nightmare to be over I wish I could make thing how they were before you hurt me embrace your mistake we are all prone to err at some point in life.

but it only when we embrace our wrongdoing just like a child just like a child how I wish too trust in life no question asked hanging on god words confident and relaxed just like a child how I long for conscience as mild as the breeze having good will with others and always of peace just like a child how I long for courage that laugh how I long for courage that laugh at fear knowing I would surely be caught when tossed in the air just like a child how I wish to take life journey with ease jolly through thick and thin as cool as you please just like child now I need this grace so dear lords you too I come help me too believe and receive your kingdom just like child conquer your daily struggle the un wasted life peace fill heart of person.

Sometime just live life because everybody not going be friend just live pretend that just life. Just in world by side have lot friend care about not my family they love me but still not my family go family to gathering that they have but I feel like out place .but I ask myself why can have family like that love me for what

I am not what want to be I am strong and wise much better but I made it wouldn't made it lose my mind one day my family see good what I did in my life .god on show

me favored in my life I know people talk about me behind my back just ask god help somebody when they I need don't be tried hurt them I tried help them but they say talk about them but

I don't sometime cuss me out call me slow fat ugly but it ok been call that all my life but

I use to it just worlds be hurt me sometime I cry too myself like in corner like did some wrong that how my mom treating me over be treat all my life but it ok people had took from me told lie on me but it ok still live I didn't finish school but I learned over the years than make it I got wise with order I got lord help me because I'm tired of dis stuff because it devil try attack me all in my circumstance because not worthy it just

CHAPTER 10

LIGHTS

Light up the way of me. I'm scared of the dark. Illuminate the blackest road with the brightest spark, light up my mind when I'm feeling low help me keep the dark thoughts away and make my mind glow, light up my worlds with your beautiful carefree smile, keep away everything that is evil, everything that is scary and vile, light up my candle when I'm out to wander and roam so no matter how far I am I may always return.

The life of a soldier

We have and understanding you and I we sit in silence nothing need to be said I know the weight you catty you hold your head high but inside you cry the life of a soldier is not an easy one memories haunt you but you stand tall and show no fear the life of a soldier is not an easy one you heard voice of days past come rushing to your head you think to yourself he was he was a good one why is he dead you wonder if you should have done thing differently no time to think only react the life of a soldier is not easy one the guilt is too much too bear although you were wounded you question why him and not me you can't forget the face that were there the life e of a soldier is not an easy one we have understanding you and I you're a soldier for life and it has not been an easy one all my life want own house nice car and swim pool in my back they all dream but hope that god will reveal all that too me because I'm just tired of struggled with my life want everything I want trip explored of world it ok but I hope that I get my publish when I can living good living life I hope that I get my wish, I will try hard to get my book published when I can living good life I hope it will go through I had hard life when I were child and since been grownup I hoping that give full blessed too me I hope prayer that I receive it because I did deserve better in life I hope one day be send my book to prison for t h e lady in there, to show them long journal of process, but seek god will it will be bless to you and god before I become strong I knew what it was like to be weak how difficult it is to love yourself to find the wholeness that you seek before I knew the light I have had my fair share of darkness too where my world fall into a hopelessness and I didn't know how to get through, for I have known the tear it take the courage to stand up against when you are broken down and bruised and you know nothing but

>The strong girl I ever knew
>She never got asked to dance or to go to prom
>She never got the chance to forget where she came from
>She never got kiss a man she idolized she never felt love bliss Cause she was paralyzed she never got talk about love with a smile
>She never got walk down church aisle she never got too say those precious word s

I do but she was far and away the strong girl I ever knew she couldn't clasp her hand as if in the Form of prayer she couldn't understanding why she was in wheeler she never showed her fear

Or let your hear her cried she never looked for pity or sympathy from you that why she I'll always be the strongest girl I ever knew

Mr., Mrs. Sims, me and my daughter joined the church, but some happened with left with my boys we keep going too church with them they pick us up and take us home Renee fisher was always around to help us with things we need she's a big sister to me. When I call Renee fisher she will come. I am thankful for my Pastors and life and Renee because always had and relied on them even do with my Baby daddy always had put my life on hold make somebody else happy, but its ok God steps in to help me with this. When can I be free from the prison of my mind? But it ok too I wish be free from man do what they say said lord help but It ok too I wish be free man do what they say said lord help me please I need it just want Be free everything live normal life have be with family tired do god will try stay bless in it but I can't people always down me when I can't come up with my life one step will start Each journey one hope to make ship one love one friend is all one heart that kind and true Friend one love one friend is all you need it really up to you.

CHAPTER 11

YOU WILL NEVER SEE ME FALL

You may see me struggle but you won't see my fall regardless if I'm weak or not. I'm going to stand tall everyone say life is easy but truly living it is not time get bard people struggle and constantly get put on the spot I'm going to wear the biggest smile even though I want to cry though I'm destined to die and even though its hard and I may struggled though it hard and it all you may see struggled but you will never see me fall.

MOM THE REFLECTION OF WOW

Mom, you are the reflection of wow.
You change sadness into happiness.
You change anger into smile.

Mom you are the reflection of wow.
You are a nurse and a cook.
You are a teacher and a housekeeper you are organizer and planner.
Mom you are the reflection of wow
you join broken heart and motivate them
you change every tear into a smile
You are the brightest star in my darkness night
Mom you are the reflection of wow you love deeply.
You care deeply, you motivate deeply

Mom you are the reflection of wow,
You are a wonderwoman
there is no person stronger, wiser, or more dedicated than a mother.

HURTING

Lying in bed my eyes resisting to close thought and anger.
I try to dispose thought of you stain my mind so many question with answer I cannot find hurt and confused as to why you'd always say you love me, But that was a repetitive lie I gave you all my love, but it wasn't enough, breaking my heart you though it made you thought I don't know what it is that you gain when you pushed me around and see me in pain do you feel empowered? Do to you that was so wrong you ripped and shattered my soul now all soul now all that left of my heart is one giant hole, nothing but emptiness and darkness take its place my heart vanished without a trace.

Peace fill heart

Once I dreamed I was walking alone the shore at lowest tide.
However I did not walk alone for stranger was on my side
I stopped and looked besides me
In eye I saw my life all time of joy and love the moment of sorrow
and hope for a moment
I was dazzled not knowing what to think in his eye
I read a riddle refining heaven with every wink.
I'm just a ripple in the endless space a minor spark
from the sea of light in the water an untraceable drop out of the forest
I looked more closely at the smaller leaf but in that wink
I am the space in the spark the heart of the light in drag
I am vast as the ocean I am the breathe of the deepest

forest
   I look more closely at our track and saw it was just one specifically of trouble point of my path his step.
   Were gone I then said stranger why?
   When I needed you the most wasn't able to see light. On the heaviest of my path the stranger viewed me with his love and replied too my request my dear child when
   It was difficult I carried you nonetheless.

Have A Good Day

May your blessing be many and your trouble be few,
And may you feel God's presence in all you say and do,
   May your Family surround you and give you reason to smile may your friends and Loved Ones go with you and extra miles, may you know joy and gladness and have a life of peace and may your load grow lighter and all your cares decrease may Your sleep be ever so sweet as you retired each night, and night and when you Retired each night and when you wake each morning may your burden feel light. May mercy and grace follow you every minute of every day and may you feel The love of god as you go on your way it really up too you one words can start a friendship, one kiss a love affair, one smile can bring you laughter, one hug can show you care, one wave of your hand can say hello, one tear can make you cry, one gentle Touch can warm a heart, one dream can make you fly, one song can bring back memories,
   One thought can see brighter days, one wish can bring colorful rainbows, one good dead can bring you Praise, one moon can light your darkness, one star can guide your soul.

AS ONE

It's okay to miss you.
It's okay to cry, just know
I'll never forget you
this isn't a permanent goodbye

Sometime I sit and wonder
If you are standing by my side
Giving me the courage to carry on with pride.
I'll hold onto our memories until this life is done.
In my heart is where I'll store them where we can be as one.

The storms of life

You may have had to suffer grief in all kinds of trails, these have come so that the proven genuineness of your faith may result in praise glory and honor. When Jesus Christ is people who face painful trails and trouble in their lives can feel Defeated as they experience the sorrow of wearing the truth is that you don't have Faith in the darkness of trouble then it is not enough of the light of good time we all Grow weary in the battle of this life once you fully understanding that Gods plan was put in place long before he formed the world, you can have knowing that he prepared a Way to take you though I am weary with moaning every night I flood my bed with tears.

Thought of the broken

I want to cry, I want to scream,
I want to tell you mostly,
I hate that I'm so afraid of everything, I hate
that you're the one thing I want the most but
can't have, I hate that you let me go before I
even got to say goodbye, I wish that you
would come back to me,
I wish I were strong enough to say no to you, I wish

that you could believe my own lie I used to cover up
the pain you left. I need to move on say my head,
my head I need to decide, says my mind, I envy her I envy the fact you
don't understand what this feel like at all I want to hurt you, I want to
be with you, I want this nightmare to be over I wish I could make
thing how they were before you hurt me.

I wish I would have given you the letter when I wanted, I need you out of my thought, I need to start doing thing for me, I hate that gave you something I can never have back. I hate that I wasted it with you I'm tired of wanting something I can't have.

I'm tired of hurting me for thing that aren't my fault I'm sorry I couldn't make you happy.

Funny thought how you never once said sorry for hurting me for breaking me for not loving me.

IN GOD EYES

In G od's eye we all make mistake .but we are still
Wonderful we all do thing that can hurt other like lying cheating or cussing in god eyes we are capable of doing good.no matter what we say
God know we can in god eyes we all just have to have faith too know that we Can success we just have to understanding that god is with us till the end we
All through something whether it's with finances family problem school. Or on the jobGod know that we can all overcome obstacle god gives us the strength to do
To what we have to do to get over those obstacles in god eye we are all children it we sin allWe have to do is ask to be forgiven in god eye some of us are flower that have been Trampled on by the devil we have had no water to grow but god is our water
And to him we all can accomplish all thing in god eyes we all overcome with god weCan overcome all thing

Searching for my soul

In this life I once felt hope I sometimes still believe in this but each moment a little Less I feel abandoned in my despair and its difficult too repair and its difficult too repair

I get broken each dat some more keeping these emotion in my core I find myself hiding behind this smile the one that show my denial I have thougth of lonesomeness which no person should poesses I camouflage this so well I feel like 1,m in hell I hurt on the insides trying to push these demons aside lwant something better tp not feel all this terror I know it can be manageable there are thing that make life tolerable ijust cannot find the thrill like 1,m undoubtedly fallible I wish to find myself soon this feel as if 1,m trapped in cocoon I would like too hatch not be so detached I need to end this coldness before death leave me soulless

Once when I was little I was happy and carefree I used too run around laugthing unit it was time for teaI used to feel on top of the worlds iused to free fine it amazine how thing change when people let you down and how that once happy face turn into solemn frown you search for someone who care anyone who understanding anyone who dare loneliness it hurt it kill you deep insides it make you feel deep insides it make you feel empty it stop you in your strides you cry yourself too sleep hugging your pillow tight wishing for someone to hold you through the night one when I was little I was happy and carefree now my lfe full of sadness pain and misery once when I was little I wa never on my own but now I pray at night I wish I

www.ingramcontent.com/pod-product-compliance
Lightning Source LLC
LaVergne TN
LVHW041543060526
838200LV00037B/1125